Breaking the Cycle
How to Elect Leaders Who Serve Us, Not Themselves
By John Nowinsky

Dedication

To my mom and dad who inspired me to be the man I have become.

To God who has reached out to me numerous times and said I have job for you and by accepting I have found my life go in directions I never would have imagined.

About The Author

Hi, my name is John Nowinsky. Rather, than bore you with the details of my personal life.

I want to take a moment and share with you how I got to this place in my life.

I answered God's calling upon life to become a caregiver at a memory assisted living facility. Yes, I moved away from a career in computer and accounting but when you answer God's calling. Life takes on new meaning and fulfillment.

There is no greater pleasure than making a difference in the life of someone. That one on one connection is a blessing for me and the one I'm with at that moment.

God has now called on me to write these books so that I can continue helping to make a difference in the lives of others.

Table Of Contents

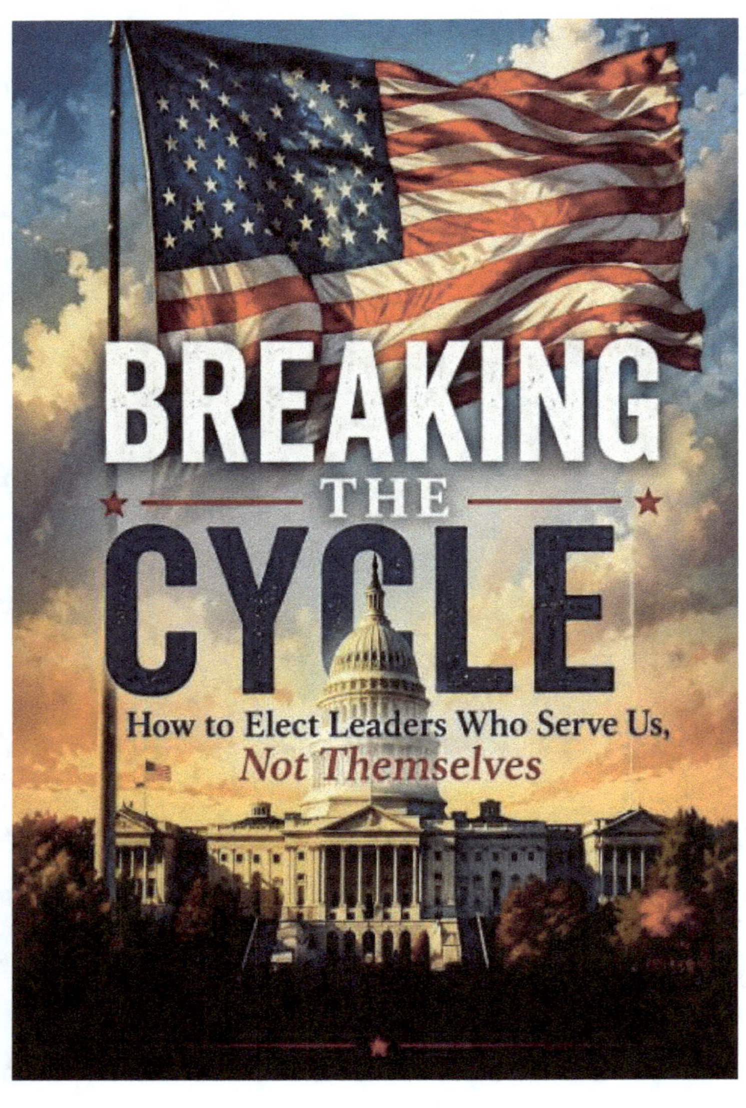

Introduction

Apathy, Disillusionment, and a Glimmer of Hope

Have you ever slammed your fist on the table in frustration, the political pundit's voices blurring into a melody of empty promises and partisan bickering? Do you find yourself scrolling past endless campaign ads featuring impossibly white teeth and carefully curated smiles, the slick slogans failing to ignite even a flicker of genuine belief? You're not alone. Millions of Americans share a growing sense of disillusionment with the political landscape. We crave strong leadership, a captain to navigate the complexities of our times. But what if the very charisma and confidence that initially attracts us masks a more troubling reality?

The Siren Song of Leaders with Narcissistic Traits

(It's important to note that this book is not intended to diagnose clinical narcissism. Our focus is on identifying leadership styles that exhibit narcissistic traits in a political context.)

Narcissistic leaders can be captivating figures. They radiate an undeniable magnetism, weaving narratives of greatness and exceptionalism like a siren's song, luring us ever closer. Their speeches are peppered with bold pronouncements and audacious claims, often promising a return to a mythical golden age – a time conveniently absent from historical records. Think of a leader who constantly invokes a past era of national glory, conveniently glossing over the realities of that time for the majority of the population. Yet, beneath the surface of charm often lurks a self-serving agenda. These individuals prioritize their own power and prestige above the needs of the people they claim to represent. Masters of manipulation, they deploy empty promises and divisive rhetoric to secure their place at the helm, leaving a trail of broken trust and fractured societies in their wake.

The Corrosive Consequences

The consequences of leadership dominated by narcissistic traits are dire. Our democratic institutions weaken as checks and balances are eroded, like a once-mighty fortress crumbling under siege. Progress stalls on critical issues as these become mere pawns in a political game of scoring points, a childish competition that leaves the real problems unattended. The needs of the most vulnerable are sacrificed at the altar of self-aggrandizement, cast aside like offerings to a false idol. Important issues are reduced to political theater, opportunities for grandstanding and manipulating public outrage rather than genuine attempts to find solutions. Foreign policy becomes unpredictable and erratic, driven by the leader's whims rather than a coherent national strategy, a rudderless ship tossed about by the currents of the leader's ego. International alliances fray, and the global stage becomes a platform for self-promotion instead of collaborative problem-solving.

Apathy's Peril: Why We Can't Afford to Be Silent

In the face of such a disheartening reality, it's tempting to succumb to apathy, to curl up in the fetal position and hope the storm passes. We might reason, perhaps with justification, that our voices won't be heard anyway. The system feels rigged, the game seemingly predetermined. But this resignation, this retreat from civic engagement, is precisely what leaders with these narcissistic traits crave. They thrive on a disengaged populace, an electorate easily manipulated by fear-mongering and manufactured outrage.

But Here's the Good News: We Can Break the Cycle

Here's the good news: we don't have to be passive bystanders in this drama. Breaking the Cycle is not just a book, it's a call to action. It's a call to reclaim our power as citizens, to shed the cloak of apathy, and to step forward as architects of a better future. Within these pages, you'll find the tools and knowledge necessary to identify the hallmarks of leadership styles with narcissistic traits. We'll dive into the psychology behind such behavior, deconstructing the tactics employed to manipulate and exploit public sentiment. More importantly, we'll empower you to become an advocate for ethical governance. You'll learn how to hold your leaders accountable, separate genuine leadership from self-serving theatrics, and champion policies that serve the collective good.

A Brighter Future Beckons: The Power of Informed Citizens

Imagine a political landscape where leaders prioritize collaboration over confrontation, where empathy guides policy decisions, and where the pursuit of power serves a greater purpose. This brighter future is within reach, but it requires informed and engaged citizens. Breaking the Cycle is your roadmap to achieving that vision. Start reading today and unleash the power within. Together, we can rewrite the narrative and elect leaders who truly embody the spirit of service, leaders who understand that their greatness lies not in self-aggrandizement, but in the collective progress they help us achieve.

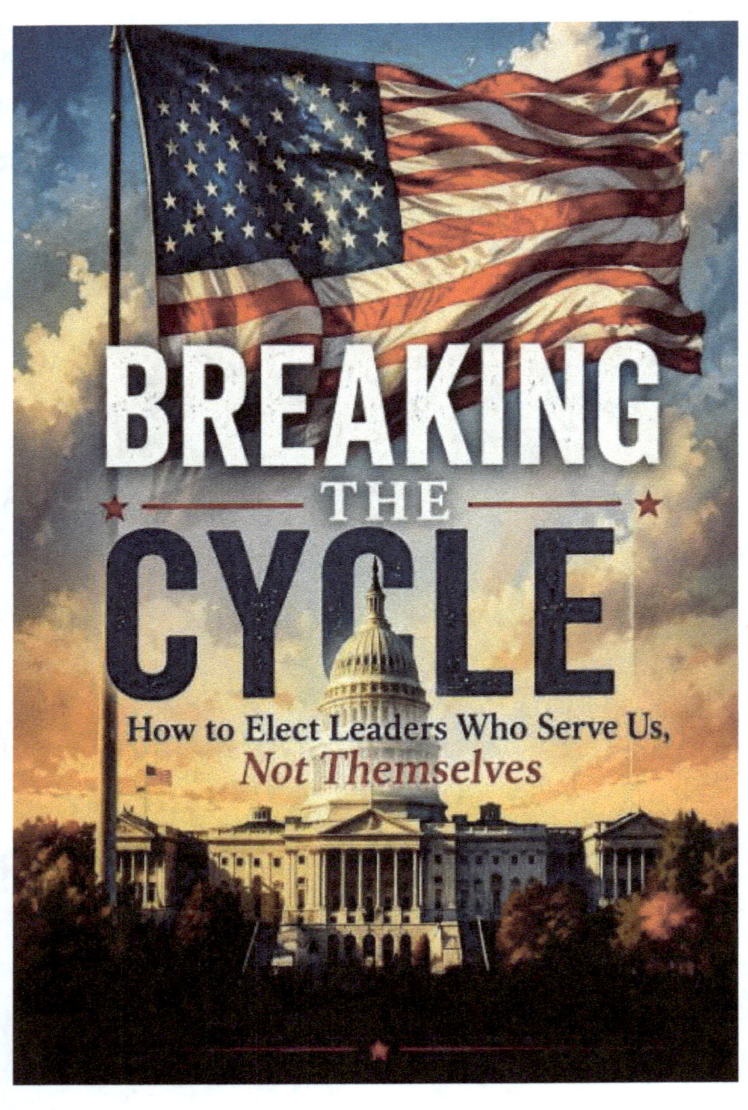

Part 1
The Narcissist's Siren Song

Chapter 1
Charisma & Control

We all crave strong leadership, someone with a vision and unwavering resolve to navigate the churning seas of our times. But what if that captivating charisma, that air of unshakeable confidence, masks a more insidious reality? This chapter dives into the troubling phenomenon of narcissistic leadership, exploring the psychological roots of the need for absolute power and unwavering admiration that compels these individuals into the political arena.

The Narcissistic Personality: A Hunger for Adoration

At the heart of narcissistic leadership lies a complex personality disorder characterized by a cluster of core traits. The most prominent of these is grandiosity, an inflated sense of self-importance and a deep-seated belief in one's own exceptionalism. Grandiose narcissists view themselves as superior beings deserving of special treatment and endless admiration. They crave constant validation, a relentless hunger for praise and recognition that can never be satiated. Imagine a bottomless pit of self-importance, forever demanding to be filled with the adoration of others. This insatiable need for validation fuels a profound sense of entitlement. Narcissistic leaders believe they are owed privileges and opportunities that others must toil for. Rules and regulations don't apply to them; they exist on a higher plane, exempt from the constraints that bind ordinary people.

Perhaps the most dangerous aspect of narcissism, in a political context, is a profound lack of empathy. Narcissists struggle to understand or care about the needs and emotions of others. They see people not as fellow human beings, but as instruments, pawns to be manipulated in their grand pursuit of power and control. Empathy is a foreign concept, a weakness they cannot afford in their ruthless climb to the top.

The Political Theater: Toxic Charisma Takes Center Stage

These core personality traits take on a particularly dangerous dimension in the political sphere. The narcissist's insatiable thirst for admiration translates into a relentless pursuit of public adulation. They cultivate an image of strength and decisiveness, often simplifying complex issues into digestible narratives that resonate with voters yearning for easy answers. Here, the concept of "toxic charisma" comes into play. Narcissistic leaders possess an undeniable magnetism, a captivating stage presence that can hold audiences spellbound. They employ grand gestures, theatrical pronouncements, and cultivate an aura of confidence that borders on arrogance.

Master storytellers, they weave compelling narratives that exploit people's fears and frustrations. They tap into a deep-seated desire for a savior figure, a charismatic leader who promises to restore order and national pride. These narratives often paint a picture of national decline, scapegoating external threats or minority groups for the very problems the narcissist themselves are ill-equipped to solve.

History's Rogues' Gallery: William Randolph Hearst and the Power of the Press

American history offers a chilling example of how narcissistic leadership can manifest outside the traditional political sphere. William Randolph Hearst, the flamboyant newspaper magnate of the late 19th and early 20th centuries, built a media empire fueled by sensationalism and exaggeration. His relentless pursuit of circulation led him to publish wildly embellished stories, often bordering on outright fabrication, to whip readers into a frenzy. Hearst's outsized personality and insatiable hunger for recognition fueled his relentless crusade to be the most powerful figure in the media landscape. His tactics, while not involving military conquest, demonstrate how a charismatic but narcissistic leader can manipulate public opinion and distort reality for personal gain, even leading the United States to war with Spain based on fabricated stories.

Modern Day Demagogues: The Allure and the Trap

Contemporary politics is not immune to the siren song of the narcissist. Some contemporary political figures have garnered significant followings by leveraging social media platforms to bypass traditional media filters and cultivate a carefully curated image that resonates with their base. These leaders excel at public displays of confidence, dismissing criticism with bombast and deflection. Opponents are not simply rivals; they are enemies, a constant threat to their perceived dominance. This tactic, framing political discourse as "us vs. them," effectively stokes fear and division, further solidifying the narcissist's position as the protector of their chosen identity group.

Case Study: Donald J. Trump - A Charismatic Façade

Donald J. Trump, the 45th president of the United States, provides a closer-to-home example of a leader who embodied many traits associated with narcissism. His rise to political power was fueled by a potent cocktail of charisma, self-promotion, and a talent for connecting with a specific segment of the electorate. Trump's signature style relied heavily on bombastic pronouncements, delivered with an air of unwavering conviction. He reveled in outlandish statements and outrageous claims, often couching them in populist rhetoric that resonated with voters yearning for a political outsider who would "drain the swamp" of Washington corruption.

His social media presence was a masterclass in cultivating a carefully curated image. Bypassing traditional media filters, he tweeted directly to his base, fostering a sense of intimacy and bypassing critical scrutiny. His tweets were peppered with self-aggrandizement, portraying him as a fearless leader battling a rigged system. He excelled at weaving narratives of national decline, tapping into anxieties about globalization and economic disenfranchisement. Opponents were routinely demonized as weak, corrupt, or out of touch with the needs of "real Americans." This strategy effectively polarized the political landscape, solidifying his position as the champion of the forgotten working class.

However, beneath the veneer of bravado lurked a leader with a demonstrably thin skin and a pathological need for praise. Criticism was met with vicious personal attacks and a relentless quest to delegitimize any dissenting voice. Policy pronouncements were often erratic and contradictory, driven more by a desire to dominate the news cycle than by a well-defined governing philosophy. His lack of empathy was evident in his policies separating migrant families at the border and his repeated downplaying of the severity of the COVID-19 pandemic. The Trump presidency serves as a cautionary tale, highlighting the dangers of electing a leader whose narcissism overshadows their qualifications and commitment to serving the greater good.

A Counterpoint: The Unifying Spirit of Barack Obama

Fortunately, charisma is not a double-edged sword. It can also be a powerful force for unity and progress.Look no further than Barack Obama, the 44th President of the United States. Obama's presidency exemplified the positive potential of charisma. His eloquence and genuine empathy resonated with millions of Americans yearning for unity and progress. He possessed a remarkable ability to articulate a shared vision for the future, inspiring a sense of collective purpose that transcended racial and political divides. Unlike narcissistic leaders who exploit fear, Obama used his charisma to promote hope and a belief in America's potential. He united the country behind ambitious goals like healthcare reform, demonstrating that charisma, coupled with a commitment to the greater good, can be a catalyst for positive change.

Beyond the Glitz: The Peril of Mistaking Charisma for Leadership

The allure of a charismatic leader can be powerful, but it's crucial to distinguish between genuine charisma and the manipulative tactics of a narcissist. True charisma is more than just charm or confidence; it's the ability to inspire others with a shared vision and purpose. It's about lifting people up, uniting them towards a common goal, rather than exploiting their fears and anxieties for personal gain.

Sharpening Your Critical Eye: Deception Unmasked

The next time you encounter a political speech or interview, pay close attention to the speaker's language and demeanor. Look for signs that might indicate narcissistic tendencies. Do they spend an inordinate amount of time praising themselves and their achievements? Do they constantly frame political discourse in terms of "us vs. them," demonizing their opponents? Most importantly, do they offer substantive solutions to complex problems, or are their pronouncements filled with empty promises and nationalistic fervor?

By honing your critical thinking skills and developing a discerning eye, you can become a more informed and engaged citizen. Recognizing the red flags of narcissism in political leaders empowers you to make informed choices at the ballot box.

Empowering the Citizen: Beyond This Chapter

Understanding the narcissist's motivations is the first step towards recognizing their deceptive tactics. Now that we've explored the dark side of charisma, the next chapter dives into the narcissist's playbook. We'll dissect the cunning strategies they employ to win at all costs, analyzing their methods for manipulating public perception and consolidating power. Equipped with this knowledge, you'll be better prepared to identify the wolves in sheep's clothing and support leaders who prioritize the collective good over their own insatiable hunger for adoration.

So, let's turn the page and dive deeper into the narcissist's playbook, learning to recognize the wolves in sheep's clothing and identify the true leaders who can guide us through complex times.

Chapter 2
The Grandiose Game

We've peeled back the layers of the narcissist's psyche, exposing the insatiable hunger for admiration and the ruthless pursuit of power that fuel their actions. But how does this personality translate into the tangible world, particularly the cutthroat arena of political campaigning? This chapter dives into the narcissist's playbook, a ruthless set of strategies designed to win at all costs. Here, we'll dissect their tactics, analyze the psychological manipulation behind them, and ultimately, empower you to see through the carefully constructed facade.

The Art of the Persona: Weaving a Spell of Charisma

Imagine a political candidate who bursts onto the scene with an aura of larger-than-life confidence. They speak with unwavering conviction, their pronouncements laced with bold promises and a touch of the dramatic. This captivating persona is a narcissist's most potent weapon. They cultivate an image of strength, decisiveness, and a unique connection to the people's needs. Think of it as a carefully crafted story, where the narcissist is the hero destined to save the day.

The psychological manipulation at play here is twofold. First, it taps into the natural human desire for a strong leader, a charismatic figure who embodies a sense of control and certainty in a world rife with complexities. Second, it fosters a sense of intimacy between the candidate and the voter. These leaders often bypass traditional media filters, utilizing social media platforms to project an image of being "one of the people," someone who understands the struggles of the ordinary citizen.

Grandiose Promises: A Castle Built on Sand

Empty promises are another hallmark of the narcissist's campaign strategy. They excel at painting a picture of a utopia just beyond reach, a future where all problems will be solved with a single stroke of their genius. These promises are often grandiose, broad enough to appeal to a wide range of voters but lacking any concrete details on how they'll be achieved. The narcissist thrives on ambiguity, for specifics can be inconvenient when accountability comes knocking.

The psychological impact of these grandiose promises is potent. They stir hope in disillusioned voters, offering a glimmer of a brighter tomorrow. In a world burdened by complexities, the simplicity of such pronouncements can be seductive. However, it's crucial to remember that these promises are often rooted not in a genuine desire to improve people's lives, but in a desperate need for adoration and a constant validation of the narcissist's perceived greatness.

Demonizing the Opposition: The Politics of Us vs. Them

One of the narcissist's most insidious tactics is the demonization of opponents. Political discourse becomes a battlefield, with the narcissist painting themselves as the sole champion of the people against a tide of evil forces. Opponents are not simply rivals; they are portrayed as incompetent, corrupt, or even a threat to the nation's very existence. This tactic serves a dual purpose. It deflects attention away from the narcissist's own shortcomings by creating a convenient scapegoat, and it fosters a sense of tribalism among their supporters. By framing the campaign as "us vs. them," the narcissist strengthens their own position as the protector of their chosen identity group.

The psychological manipulation here is particularly dangerous. It stokes fear and division, playing on preexisting anxieties and prejudices. It simplifies complex issues into a black-and-white narrative, leaving no room for nuance or critical thinking. In the heat of such an emotionally charged atmosphere, voters can become blind to the narcissist's true motivations and susceptible to manipulation.

Case Study: The Master of Sizzle, Not Steak - Huey Long

American history offers its own example in the rise and fall of Huey Long, the charismatic governor of Louisiana from 1932 to 1935. Long, nicknamed the "Kingfish," was a master of populist rhetoric and a skilled manipulator of public perception.

He cultivated an image as the champion of the "forgotten man," the ordinary citizen struggling against the wealthy elite and entrenched interests. His "Share the Wealth" program promised a radical redistribution of income, appealing to voters hit hard by the Great Depression. While the specifics of the program were often hazy, the emotional resonance was undeniable.

Long wasn't shy about demonizing his opponents. He portrayed himself as a lone wolf battling a corrupt political establishment in Washington. He lambasted special interests and big business, painting them as the villains responsible for the economic hardship plaguing the common man. This "us vs. them" narrative solidified his position as the defender of the downtrodden and further fueled his charismatic appeal.

However, beneath the populist veneer lurked a man with a ruthless ambition and an insatiable hunger for power. Long's "Share the Wealth" program, while capturing the public imagination, was criticized for its economic feasibility. His attacks on opponents often turned personal and vindictive. As his political influence grew, he increasingly resorted to strongman tactics, silencing dissent and consolidating control.

Huey Long's story serves as a cautionary tale. His rise to power demonstrates the potent allure of a charismatic leader who promises simple solutions to complex problems. However, it also highlights the dangers of unchecked ambition and the manipulation of populist anger for personal gain. Long's grand promises and demonization of opponents served to mask a deeper agenda, one that prioritized his own power over the true needs of the people.

Seeing Through the Smoke and Mirrors: Critical Thinking as Your Weapon

So, how do we, the discerning voters, recognize these tactics and avoid falling prey to them? The first step is to sharpen our critical thinking skills. When a candidate bombards you with empty promises, ask yourself: how exactly will they achieve these goals? What is their track record on similar issues? Look beyond the charisma and the carefully crafted soundbites. When an opponent is demonized, pay attention to the language used. Are they being criticized for their policies or simply attacked on a personal level?

The next time you encounter a political advertisement, dissect the message it conveys. What visuals are used? Are they designed to evoke fear or a sense of national pride? Does the ad focus on the candidate's qualifications or rely on emotional manipulation? By becoming more aware of these tactics,

The narcissist's campaign playbook thrives in the shadows. By understanding their tactics, we can become empowered citizens, less susceptible to manipulation and more discerning in our evaluation of political candidates. Remember, true leadership is not about self-aggrandizement or empty promises. It's about a genuine commitment to public service, a willingness to engage in constructive dialogue, and a dedication to building a better future for all, not just a select few.

In the next chapter, we'll dive deeper into the narcissist's bag of tricks, exploring their manipulation of language and the media to control the narrative. By understanding their rhetorical strategies, we can become more informed voters, capable of identifying the substance behind the bluster.

Chapter 3
Promises & Pitfalls: When Words Don't Mean What They Say

Ever feel bombarded by political ads promising a utopia overnight? Let's call this politician Senator Smoothtalker. They pledge to fix the economy, rebuild infrastructure in a flash, and launch us to Mars by next Tuesday. Sounds like a dream, right? But beware! This chapter dives into how manipulative politicians use empty promises to win votes.

The Art of the Impossible Promise: When Fantasy Outpaces Reality

Narcissists are masters of crafting grand pronouncements. They paint a picture-perfect future where every problem has a simple solution, all thanks to their brilliant leadership, of course. These promises are often so outlandish, so disconnected from reality, that it's tempting to dismiss them entirely. But that's where the manipulation kicks in. They exploit our deepest desires and frustrations, dangling the promise of a quick fix like a shiny object. We get mesmerized by the solution without considering how realistic it actually is.

Scapegoating: The Blame Game Never Ends

But what happens when those impossible promises inevitably fail to materialize? When Senator Smoothtalker's utopia remains out of reach? Enter the narcissist's other favorite tactic: scapegoating. Suddenly, it's not their fault. It's the bureaucrats, the special interests, or even a freak snowstorm (yes, you read that right) that conspired to derail their brilliant plans. This finger-pointing serves two purposes. It deflects blame away from the narcissist, protecting their ego, and it fuels a sense of "us vs. them" among their supporters. By identifying a common enemy, they solidify their own position as the sole protector.

Fear and Urgency: Playing on Our Emotions

Another weapon in the narcissist's arsenal is emotional manipulation. They might paint a nightmarish picture of the future if their opponent wins, stoking anxieties about everything from economic collapse to national security threats. Or, they might create a sense of urgency, claiming there's a limited window to solve a crisis, pressuring voters into rash decisions based on fear. It's like that feeling you get during a "flash sale" – you might not need that extra toaster oven, but the fear of missing out compels you to buy it anyway.

Case Study: Donald Trump's 2016 Presidential Campaign (A Word of Caution)

It's important to remember that political issues are complex. While the 2016 campaign of Donald Trump serves as a clear example of the tactics discussed here, it's not the only narrative. Simple explanations rarely capture the full picture.

That said, Trump's campaign was undeniably built on bold promises and divisive rhetoric. One of his signature promises – a wall along the US-Mexico border funded by Mexico – was a cornerstone of his campaign, but unrealistic from the start. He also heavily relied on scapegoating immigrants for the country's problems. This resonated with some voters feeling disenfranchised. Trump's strategy was to create urgency and fear among his supporters. By making vague and unrealistic promises, he positioned himself as the only one who could solve America's problems. This message resonated with many voters. However, hindsight reveals a campaign built on shaky ground. Promises were often based on flawed assumptions or outright lies, and the scapegoating tactics were harmful and divisive. This case study serves as a reminder of the importance of critical thinking and fact-checking in evaluating political rhetoric.

So, How Do We See Through the Smoke and Mirrors?

Alright, informed voters, how do we avoid falling prey to these tactics? First, let's sharpen our critical thinking skills. When a politician throws out a seemingly impossible promise, ask yourself: is there a clear plan for achieving it? What are the potential roadblocks? Research their past record – have they delivered on promises before? Look beyond the emotional appeals and carefully crafted soundbites. A genuine leader focuses on outlining practical solutions, not fear-mongering or assigning blame.

Promises vs. Policies: Fact-Checking the Fine Print

Remember Senator Smoothtalker's promise to rebuild infrastructure overnight? Let's say their opponent, Candidate Clearview, proposes a more detailed plan that focuses on public-private partnerships, utilizes sustainable materials, and emphasizes long-term maintenance. Sure, it might not sound as flashy, but it has a higher chance of actually being implemented. The key here is to differentiate between a policy proposal with concrete steps and a hollow promise that relies on smoke and mirrors. Websites like PolitiFact or FactCheck.org can be helpful resources for verifying the accuracy of campaign claims.

Beyond the Hype: Looking for Substance

This chapter might leave you feeling a tad cynical, but don't despair! There are genuine leaders out there who focus on building trust, engage in constructive dialogue, and prioritize the well-being of their citizens over their own egos. By developing a critical eye and doing your research, you can see through the narcissist's manipulative tactics and support candidates who offer genuine solutions, not just empty promises. Here are some additional tips:

Look for leaders who prioritize substance over charisma. Charisma can be intoxicating, but don't be swayed by style over experience and practical solutions.

Seek out candidates who focus on common ground. Divisive rhetoric may be loud, but genuine leaders understand the importance of compromise and working together for the greater good.

Attend town halls and debates. These events offer a chance to see how candidates handle themselves under pressure and respond to tough questions. You can assess their authenticity and ability to think on their feet.

Consider the long game. Don't get caught up in short-term promises or emotional appeals. Think about the candidate's vision for the future and how their policies will impact your community in the long run.

By following these tips and staying informed, you can become a more discerning voter and hold your elected officials accountable. Remember, a healthy democracy relies on an active and engaged citizenry. So get out there, research the candidates, and cast your vote for the leader who you believe will truly represent your values and best interests.

But what happens when someone sweeps you off your feet not with grand political promises, but with an overwhelming display of affection and attention? This intense initial connection, often seen in abusive relationships, is exactly what we'll explore in the next chapter.

Chapter 4
Love Bombing the Public: When Politicians Shower You with Affection (But Not Policy)

Ever scroll through social media and feel this weird connection with a politician you've never met? They're all about your values, showering you with praise and promising unwavering support for everything you care about. It's a powerful feeling, this sense of belonging and fierce loyalty. But what if this intense emotional connection, the kind you see in bad relationships, is being used to manipulate you when it comes to voting?

This chapter dives into "love bombing," a tactic narcissists use to create dependence and loyalty. We'll explore how this manipulative strategy goes beyond dating and infiltrates the political sphere, potentially influencing who you vote for.

Love Bombing: A Political Weapon

Love bombing is basically an emotional blitz. It's like overwhelming someone with affection, flattery, and promises of never letting them down. In a political context, this might translate to a candidate showering everyone with praise, singling out specific groups for tons of admiration, and making these grand promises about a utopian future they'll create. Imagine being at a rally where the candidate remembers your town's name, gushes about your local industry, and throws out campaign merch with your community slogan on it. This is a calculated move designed to trigger a powerful emotional response – feeling seen, heard, and valued.

The Entanglement: Why Love Bombing Works

The psychological impact of this tactic is undeniable. Imagine someone telling you you're the backbone of the nation, the key to a brighter future. Imagine a politician holding rallies where they single out your community for special attention, praising your work ethic, your cultural heritage, or your unwavering patriotism. It creates a powerful sense of belonging and an unspoken obligation to reciprocate this affection with unwavering loyalty. You become invested in their success, not just for the sake of policy, but because their victory feels strangely personal.

The Charisma Conundrum: Telling Real Connection from Manipulation

But it's crucial to distinguish between healthy charisma and manipulative tactics. Real charisma is an inspiring force. It's the ability to connect with people on an emotional level, to articulate a vision that ignites passion, and to motivate others to work towards a common goal. Think of leaders who inspire hope and a sense of collective purpose. That's the power of genuine charisma.

So, how do we differentiate between authentic charisma and the manipulative tactics used by narcissists? Here are a few key distinctions:

Self-Promotion vs. Public Service: Healthy charisma inspires followers to work towards a greater good, a vision that transcends the leader themself. Narcissistic leaders, however, use charisma for self-aggrandizement. Their speeches are peppered with "I" statements, and their vision often revolves around their own perceived brilliance. They might talk about "making America great again" but offer little in the way of concrete plans on how to achieve that greatness.

Divisive Language vs. Unifying Rhetoric: Effective leaders use language that unites people towards a common goal. They acknowledge differences but emphasize shared values. Narcissists, however, thrive on division. They create an "us vs. them" mentality, using inflammatory language to pit one group against another. They might frame complex issues in a way that simplifies the problem and positions themselves as the only solution, the sole protector against a looming threat.

Empty Promises vs. Substantive Policy Proposals: Healthy charisma is often accompanied by concrete plans to achieve a vision. Leaders outline clear steps, potential roadblocks, and a realistic timeline for achieving their goals. Narcissists, on the other hand, rely on vague promises with little substance. Their solutions are often simplistic and devoid of any practical details. They might promise to "build a wall" or "drain the swamp" but offer no specifics on how these solutions would be implemented or funded.

Love Bombing in Action: A Social Media Blitz

These distinctions are crucial because love bombing thrives in an environment of emotional connection, not critical thinking. Take social media, for example. A narcissistic politician might cultivate a carefully crafted online persona. They respond to comments, answer questions directly, and create a sense of intimacy with their followers. They might hold live Q&A sessions or host lighthearted polls, all designed to foster a sense of camaraderie. They might single out specific individuals for praise, leaving comments like, "Great point, [@username]! You're exactly why I'm doing this!" This targeted flattery fosters a sense of obligation and a fierce loyalty that goes beyond policy positions.

Beyond Rallies: Decoding Campaign Speeches

Analyzing campaign rallies can also reveal the use of love bombing tactics. Watch for excessive flattery directed towards specific demographics. Listen for promises that are emotionally charged but lack concrete details. Is the focus on the leader's brilliance and past accomplishments, or on a clear plan for the future and how they'll address the challenges facing the country? Do they paint a picture of a utopia they'll single-handedly create, or do they acknowledge the complexities of governing and outline a collaborative approach? A genuine leader will focus on the collective "we" and the shared journey towards a better tomorrow, not the singular "I" and their own heroic narrative.

Case Study: Analyzing Donald Trump's Use of Love Bombing Tactics

It's important to note that interpretations of these tactics can vary depending on political viewpoints. However, examining Donald Trump's political career offers a case study in how love bombing can be used in the political sphere.

Social Media Interactions: Trump's Twitter account was a key platform for him to connect with his supporters. He frequently used tweets to express his gratitude and appreciation, often using phrases like "Thank you so much" and "I love you all." He also frequently retweeted and responded to his supporters' tweets, creating a sense of personal connection and validation.

Campaign Speeches: Trump's campaign speeches often featured him praising his supporters, calling them "amazing" and "incredible." He frequently used phrases like "We're going to win so bigly" and "We're going to make America great again," creating a sense of shared purpose and excitement. He also frequently attacked his political opponents, creating a sense of us-vs-them and reinforcing his supporters' loyalty.

Rallies: Trump's rallies were a key platform for him to connect with his supporters in person. He frequently praised his supporters, calling them "patriots" and "heroes." He also frequently used music and spectacle to create a sense of excitement and shared experience. His supporters often left his rallies feeling energized and motivated, with a strong sense of loyalty to Trump and his movement.

Analysis:

Trump's use of love bombing tactics was undeniably effective in building a loyal following. By frequently expressing gratitude and appreciation for his supporters, he created a sense of personal connection and validation. By praising his supporters and attacking his political opponents, he created a sense of shared purpose and excitement. By using music and spectacle at his rallies, he created a sense of shared experience and community.

Love bombing can be a powerful tool for manipulating voters. By understanding its tactics, we can become more discerning voters. However, the fight against political manipulation doesn't end here. In the next part, we will equip you with the tools to identify narcissistic traits in the political sphere. We'll dive into the warning signs to watch out for, the red flags that should raise an eyebrow. Empowered with this knowledge, you can become a more informed and critical voter, capable of seeing through manipulative tactics and choosing leaders who prioritize substance over spectacle.

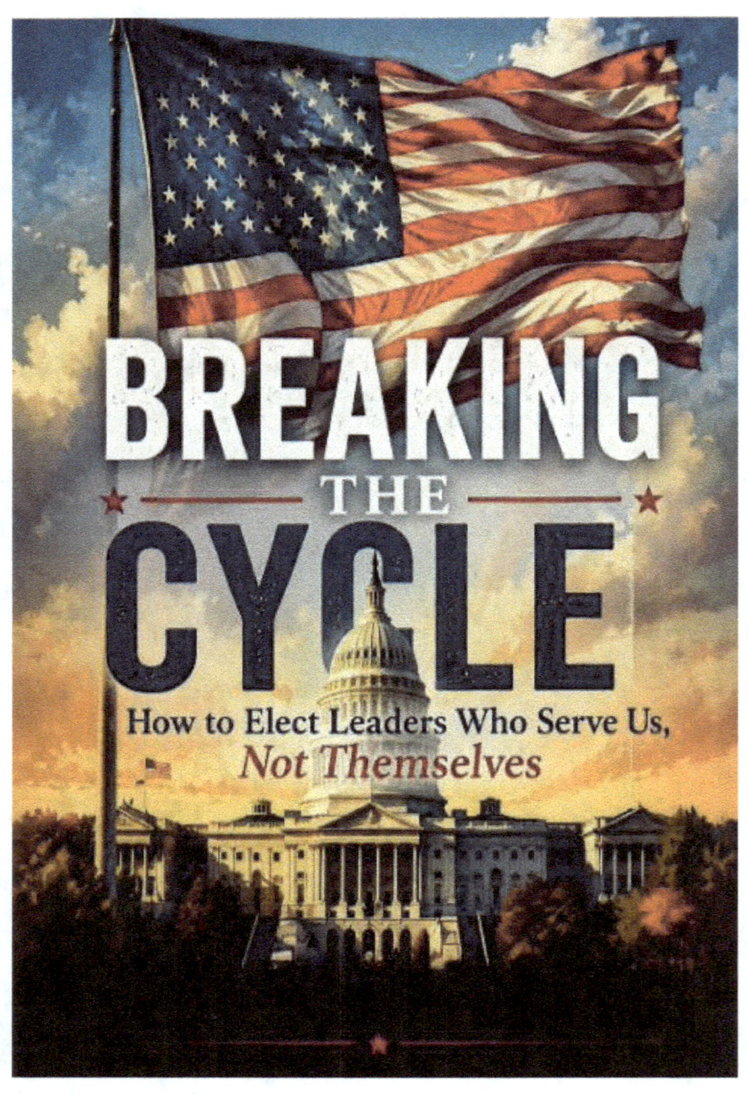

Part 2
Unmasking the Wolf in Sheep's Clothing

Chapter 5
Red Flags & Smoke Signals: Unmasking the Wolf in Sheep's Clothing

Not every charismatic leader lurking on your screen is a full-blown narcissist. But let's face it, charisma can be a double-edged sword. While it can inspire and unite, it can also be wielded to manipulate and control. So, how do we differentiate between genuine leadership and a carefully crafted performance? This chapter equips you with the tools to identify the warning signs, the red flags that might signal a narcissistic politician lurking beneath the veneer.

The Narcissistic Playbook: Key Traits to Watch Out For

Imagine a politician who craves constant praise, a never-ending chorus of "you're the best!" Imagine someone who demonizes their opponents, painting them as villains or existential threats. Now picture a leader who dismisses facts that contradict their narrative, who bends reality to fit their own image. These are just a few of the key traits that raise red flags when it comes to spotting a narcissistic politician.

Weaponizing the Media: Controlling the Narrative and Silencing Dissent

The media landscape offers a massive stage for politicians, and narcissistic leaders know how to exploit it. They cultivate relationships with certain media outlets, ensuring favorable coverage and a platform to amplify their message. Critical voices, on the other hand, are often dismissed as "fake news" or attacks from a biased media. This tactic aims to control the narrative, to drown out dissenting voices, and ultimately, to dictate how the public perceives them.

Authoritarianism's Shadow: A Threat Beyond Narcissism

It's important to note that not all threats to democracy come wrapped in a narcissistic package. Authoritarian leaders, while they might not exhibit all the classic narcissistic traits, can still pose a significant danger. They often prioritize control and centralization of power, eroding democratic institutions and stifling dissent. They might use nationalistic rhetoric or create a climate of fear to justify their actions. Regardless of their specific personality type, leaders who exhibit these authoritarian tendencies deserve a healthy dose of skepticism.

Red Flags in Action: Spotting Narcissistic Traits Through Examples

Let's dissect some real-world examples to see these red flags in action. Take, for instance, a leader who constantly boasts about their achievements, minimizing or even rewriting history to make themselves look better. This insatiable need for self-aggrandizement is a classic narcissistic trait.

Demonizing Opponents: Us vs. Them

Now consider a politician who demonizes their opponents, portraying them as enemies of the state or a threat to the nation's very fabric. This "us vs. them" mentality not only fosters division but also discourages critical thinking and constructive dialogue. It's a tactic that thrives on fear and a sense of impending danger.

Facts Be Damned: Disregard for Evidence

What about a leader who dismisses factual evidence that contradicts their narrative? They might call legitimate news sources biased or even create their own "alternative facts" to suit their agenda. This blatant disregard for truth and reality erodes trust and makes informed decision-making nearly impossible.

Empathy Deficit: A Leader Who Can't Relate

Finally, pay attention to a leader's ability (or inability) to empathize. Can they connect with the struggles and challenges faced by their constituents? Or do they seem aloof and self-absorbed, more interested in their own image than the well-being of the people they represent? A lack of empathy is a glaring red flag, especially when dealing with complex issues that require compassion and understanding.

Case Study: Analyzing Donald Trump's Response to the 2020 Presidential Election

Introduction:

Donald Trump's response to the 2020 presidential election provides a recent example of a leader displaying multiple red flags of narcissism. It's worth noting that interpretations of these actions can vary depending on political viewpoints. However, this case study will analyze Trump's behavior and rhetoric during this period, highlighting the red flags of narcissism that were on full display.

Red Flag 1: Grandiosity

Trump's response to the election was marked by grandiose claims and exaggerations. He repeatedly claimed that he had won the election in a "landslide" and that the results were "rigged" against him. These claims were baseless and unsupported by evidence, demonstrating Trump's tendency to exaggerate and distort reality to suit his own narrative.

Red Flag 2: Need for Admiration

Trump's response to the election was also marked by a need for admiration and attention. He repeatedly sought to draw attention to himself, making outlandish claims and accusations in order to stay in the spotlight. This behavior demonstrates Trump's need for constant admiration and attention, a hallmark of narcissistic personality disorder.

Red Flag 3: Lack of Empathy

Trump's response to the election showed a complete lack of

empathy for his opponents and critics. He repeatedly attacked and belittled his political opponents, including Joe Biden and Kamala Harris, demonstrating a complete disregard for their feelings and perspectives. This behavior is a clear red flag of narcissism, as it shows a lack of ability to understand and relate to others.

Red Flag 4: Entitlement

Trump's response to the election also demonstrated a sense of entitlement and expectation of special treatment. He repeatedly claimed that he had been unfairly treated by the media and the electoral system, and that he was owed the presidency. This behavior demonstrates Trump's belief that he is entitled to special treatment and that the rules do not apply to him.

Red Flag 5: Manipulation

Finally, Trump's response to the election showed a willingness to manipulate others in order to achieve his goals. He repeatedly made false claims and accusations in order to undermine the legitimacy of the election and to sow discord among his supporters. This behavior demonstrates

Trump's willingness to manipulate others in order to achieve his own ends, a clear red flag of narcissism.

Conclusion:

Donald Trump's response to the 2020 presidential election provides a clear example of a leader displaying multiple red flags of narcissism. His grandiose claims, need for admiration, lack of empathy, sense of entitlement, and willingness to manipulate others all demonstrate a narcissistic personality disorder. This case study highlights the importance of recognizing and addressing these red flags in leaders, in order to prevent harm to individuals and society as a whole.

Unveiling the Manipulation

Now that we've explored some key red flags, let's turn the spotlight on you, the discerning voter. How can you identify apolitician who prioritizes personal gain over the public good?One way is to pay attention to their policy proposals. Do these plans primarily benefit a select few or do they address the needs of the broader population? Additionally, how does the politician handle criticism? Do they engage in respectful discourse or resort to personal attacks and mudslinging?

Analyze the Rhetoric: Unmasking Manipulative Language

Narcissists are masters of language. They use words to frame issues, evoke emotions, and ultimately, influence voters. Here's a challenge: Analyze recent political speeches or interviews. Can you identify any red flags of narcissism? Here are some specific aspects to consider:

Excessive Use of "I" Statements: Look for speeches where the leader focuses heavily on their own achievements and uses phrases like "I did this" or "I created that" excessively. This constant self-promotion is a hallmark of narcissistic leadership.

Shifting Blame and Responsibility: Pay attention to how the politician handles criticism or setbacks. Do they take ownership of mistakes, or do they deflect blame and point fingers at others? A narcissistic leader will rarely accept responsibility for failures.

Vague Promises and Oversimplification: Be wary of leaders who make grand, sweeping promises with little detail on how they'll achieve them. Complex problems rarely have simple solutions, and a narcissistic leader might oversimplify issues to appear competent and decisive.

Us vs. Them Mentality: Listen for language that pits one group against another. Does the politician constantly frame issues in terms of "us" versus a dangerous "them?" This tactic thrives on fear and division, discouraging critical thinking.

Empowering Yourself: Becoming a Critical Thinker

By equipping yourself with these tools, you can become a more critical and discerning voter. Remember, elections are about choosing a leader who will represent your best interests, not simply someone who delivers a captivating performance. Don't be afraid to challenge what you hear and to seek out information from a variety of sources. A healthy democracy thrives on an engaged and informed citizenry, and that starts with you.

The Media Landscape: A Double-Edged Sword

The media plays a crucial role in shaping public perception, and narcissistic politicians understand this power all too well. In the next chapter, we will explore the tactics these leaders use to manipulate the media and control the narrative. We'll dive into issues like media bias, fake news, and the importance of critical media literacy in today's complex political landscape. By understanding these challenges, you'll be better equipped to navigate the information age and make informed decisions about the leaders you choose.

Chapter 6
Spinning the Web: How Politicians Control the Narrative

The media landscape, with its vast reach and undeniable influence, acts as a double-edged sword. It can be a platform for informing the public, a forum for fostering debate, and a watchdog holding leaders accountable. But in the hands of a skilled manipulator, the media can also be a tool for deception and control. This chapter dives into the tactics narcissistic politicians employ to use the media to their advantage, crafting narratives that paint them in a favorable light while silencing dissent.

Weaving a Narrative: Controlling the Message

Imagine a politician who meticulously stages events, ensuring they unfold like perfectly choreographed plays designed to generate positive media coverage. Now picture another who strategically leaks information to friendly media outlets, shaping the news cycle in their favor. These are just a few ways politicians manipulate the media, aiming to control the narrative and ultimately, influence public perception.

One tactic involves discrediting journalists who dare to ask critical questions. These leaders might launch personal attacks, portraying reporters as biased or even "enemies of the people." This not only discourages tough questioning but also fosters a climate of fear and intimidation within the media itself.

The Peril of Partisanship: Navigating a Biased Media Landscape

The rise of biased media outlets further complicates the issue. News sources can become echo chambers, reinforcing pre-existing beliefs and demonizing opposing viewpoints. This makes it increasingly difficult for the public to access objective information and form independent judgments.

Here's where media literacy becomes crucial. It's about understanding how information is presented, recognizing bias, and critically evaluating the sources you consume. Look for outlets that strive for factual accuracy and present a variety of perspectives. Be wary of sensational headlines and emotionally charged language designed to evoke a specific reaction. Don't be afraid to fact-check information and verify claims before accepting them as truth.

Examples: Unmasking Media Manipulation in Action

Let's dissect real-world examples to see how this manipulation unfolds. Imagine a press conference where a leader deflects questions skillfully, dodging any inquiries that might expose their shortcomings. They might resort to irrelevant tangents, whataboutism (shifting blame to others), or simply repeating pre-prepared talking points. This tactic aims to control the conversation and ensure only their preferred narrative is conveyed.

Another tactic involves staging events specifically for media consumption. Picture a leader visiting a factory floor, surrounded by cheering workers, all carefully orchestrated for a positive photo op. While the visuals might paint a picture of prosperity and leadership, the reality might be far less rosy.

Finally, consider how some leaders attack journalists who pose challenging questions. They might resort to name-calling, ridicule, or even threats, all designed to silence dissent and discourage further scrutiny. This chilling effect creates an environment where journalists are hesitant to hold power to account.

Case Studies

The Watergate Deception (or The Watergate Scandal)

In the early 1970s, the Watergate scandal exposed the dark side of power and media manipulation. The Nixon administration attempted to control the narrative surrounding a break-in at the Democratic National Committee headquarters. They employed tactics like denial, discrediting journalists, leaks and misinformation, and a PR offensive. While initially successful, relentless investigative journalism exposed the lies and highlighted the importance of a free press.

Trump and Voter Fraud Claims (or Casting Doubt: The 2020 Election)

Donald Trump's 2020 presidential campaign provides a recent example of media manipulation. He repeatedly made baseless claims of widespread voter fraud, using friendly media outlets and social media to amplify his message. This strategy aimed to sow doubt about the election's legitimacy and mobilize his base. This case study underscores the importance of critically evaluating information and seeking out multiple sources.

Discussion Prompts: Becoming a Discerning Consumer of Information

Now that we've explored these strategies, let's turn the spotlight on you, the empowered citizen. How can you distinguish between objective news reporting and political spin? Here are some tips:

Identify Sources: Pay attention to the source of the information. Is it a reputable news outlet with a history of factual reporting, or a website with a known political agenda?

Check for Bias: Look for balanced reporting that presents multiple perspectives. Does the article offer evidence to support its claims, or is it primarily based on opinion?

Beware of Emotional Triggers: Be wary of articles that rely heavily on sensational headlines or emotionally charged language designed to evoke a specific reaction.

The Power of Platforms: Social Media's Role in Shaping Public Opinion

Social media platforms play a significant role in shaping public opinion today. They allow politicians to bypass traditional media outlets and communicate directly with their base. While this fosters a sense of connection, it also presents significant challenges. Social media algorithms tend to create echo chambers, feeding users information that confirms their existing beliefs and making it difficult to encounter opposing viewpoints.

Framing the Debate: How Media Coverage Shapes Perceptions

Here's an additional challenge: Compare news coverage of different candidates from various media outlets. How does the framing of the story differ? The same event might be presented with a positive spin by one outlet and a negative spin by another. This highlights the importance of consuming information from a variety of sources and critically evaluating the framing used by each outlet.

Empowering Yourself: Becoming a Critical Consumer of Media

The good news is that you're not powerless in this information battleground. By equipping yourself with media literacy skills, you can become a more discerning consumer of information. Here are some actionable steps you can take:

Diversify Your Media Diet: Don't rely on a single source for your news. Seek out outlets with different political leanings to gain a more comprehensive understanding of current events.

Fact-Check Regularly: Don't take everything you read or see at face value. Utilize fact-checking websites and reputable sources to verify information before sharing it.

Engage in Civil Discourse: Discuss current events with people who hold different viewpoints. While respectful debate can be challenging, it can also foster critical thinking and a deeper understanding of complex issues.

Support Investigative Journalism: Investigative journalism plays a vital role in holding powerful figures accountable.

Consider supporting reputable news organizations that invest in in-depth reporting.

By following these tips, you can become a more informed and empowered citizen, less susceptible to manipulation and better equipped to navigate the intricate web of information in today's world.

Cultivating a Critical Eye

In today's media-saturated world, where charismatic personalities and soundbites dominate the airwaves, it's easy to be swayed by appearances. In the next chapter will remind us of the importance of looking beyond the surface and critically evaluating a politician's qualifications and actions, not just their charm or media presence.

Chapter 7
Beyond Celebrity Politics: Unveiling the Leader Beneath the Shine

The flickering images bombard us – a politician with a dazzling smile, delivering a speech packed with catchy slogans. In the whirlwind of the 24/7 news cycle, it's easy to get swept away by charisma. But hold on a beat, because this chapter is your wake-up call. Let's move beyond the glitz and glamour and dive deeper, because effective leadership requires a whole symphony of qualities, and charisma is just one instrument in the orchestra.

Imagine you're the captain tasked with assembling a crew for a perilous voyage – a journey fraught with unpredictable storms and uncharted territories. Would you choose the first mate with the most captivating laugh and a flair for storytelling, or the seasoned navigator with a weathered face and a deep understanding of the treacherous currents? The answer's a no-brainer, right? So why, then, do we sometimes fall short of applying that same logic to our political leaders?

This chapter is about equipping you with the tools to see beyond the smoke and mirrors. We'll be dissecting the importance of evaluating a candidate's qualifications, experience, and policy positions. These are the cornerstones of effective leadership. After all, a leader isn't just there to deliver soundbites and bask in the glow of applause; they're there to make tough calls, navigate complex issues with a steady hand, and ultimately, shape the course of our society.

History is a treasure trove of cautionary tales about the perils of being seduced by charisma alone. Remember that election where the smooth-talking candidate with zero experience in the political arena swept the polls, leaving the seasoned expert with a proven track record floundering in the dust? The ramifications of that decision might still be reverberating today.

A Tale of Two Leaders: Charisma vs. Substance

Let's bring this to life with a concrete example. Take Bill Clinton and Jimmy Carter. Clinton, undeniably charismatic, possessed an uncanny ability to connect with voters on a personal level. Carter, on the other hand, came across as more reserved, focusing on the finer details of policy and practical solutions. While Clinton's charm propelled him to electoral victories, his legacy is tarnished by scandals and a lack of focus on long-term policy solutions. Conversely, Carter, though lacking Clinton's charisma, became a champion for human rights and environmental issues, leaving a lasting positive impact on the global stage.

This comparison throws a spotlight on a crucial point: charisma can be a double-edged sword. It might win elections, but it doesn't guarantee effective leadership. Here's the million-dollar question we need to ask ourselves: Do we want a leader who can charm a room but struggles with complex challenges, or one who might not be the life of the party but possesses the knowledge and experience to navigate a crisis with wisdom and foresight?

Empowering the Citizen: Beyond the Candidate's Smile

Now, let's shift the spotlight onto you, the empowered citizen. What qualities should we truly be prioritizing in a leader? Here's a roadmap to guide you:

Experience: Does the candidate have a proven track record of accomplishment in a relevant field? Have they held positions that demanded difficult decisions and the ability to manage complex situations effectively?

Knowledge: Does the candidate possess a deep understanding of the issues facing our nation? Are they well-versed in policy details and the nuances of different perspectives?

Judgment: Can the candidate think critically, weigh evidence objectively, and make sound decisions under pressure?

Integrity: Does the candidate have a strong moral compass? Are they committed to ethical conduct and transparency in all their dealings?

Vision: Does the candidate have a clear vision for the future? Can they articulate their goals in a compelling way and inspire others to work towards them with a sense of shared purpose?

But how do we actually unearth these qualities in a candidate? There's a wealth of resources at your fingertips. Candidate websites, policy statements, and voting records are all excellent starting points. Reputable news organizations often provide in-depth profiles and analyses of candidates' positions on various issues. Don't be afraid to go the extra mile – watch interviews, attend town halls, and see how candidates handle themselves in different settings. Observe their body language, the way they answer questions, and whether they focus on solutions or simply sling mud at their opponents.

Here's an additional challenge for the truly engaged citizen: Research the voting records and policy positions of different candidates with a fine-tooth comb. What are their stances on the issues that keep you up at night? Education? Healthcare? The environment? By understanding their positions, you can truly assess if their values align with yours. Imagine it like choosing a teammate for a crucial game – wouldn't you want someone who shares your goals and strategies, someone who's going to fight alongside you for what you believe in?

Uncritical Loyalty: The Shadow of Celebrity Politics

However, there's another danger lurking in the shadows of celebrity politics: the tendency for charisma to morph into something more concerning – uncritical loyalty. Imagine a leader so captivating, so appealing, that their supporters become blind to any flaws or missteps. This is the dark side of charisma. Supporters prioritize the leader's image and pronouncements over critical thinking and accountability. Facts are dismissed, dissenting voices are silenced, and any criticism is seen as a personal attack.

This unwavering loyalty, evident in the unwavering support for Donald Trump despite scandals and divisive rhetoric, can have a crippling effect on a democracy. Healthy debate, essential for a well-functioning society, is stifled. Leaders become unaccountable, and the potential for corruption grows.

Beyond Our Borders: A Look Back in Time

Uncritical loyalty isn't exactly a new invention. Leaders throughout history have managed to inspire some pretty intense devotion, sometimes bordering on obsession. Take William Jennings Bryan, for instance. This late 19th and early 20th-century politician was a real rockstar in his day. People loved his fiery speeches and his commitment to what he believed in. But here's the thing – blind loyalty can be dangerous. Bryan ran for president three times, each time on a platform of silver coinage, which most economists considered a bad idea. While his supporters adored him, his unwavering focus on this one policy might have clouded his judgment on other crucial issues.

The point is, even charismatic leaders we admire can have blind spots. It's important to remember that and evaluate their actions critically, not just cheer them on because they're our guy.

A Chorus of Voices, Not a Solo Act

Effective leadership isn't a one-man show. A strong leader understands the importance of a diverse range of voices and perspectives. They surround themselves with advisors from different backgrounds and experiences, fostering a richer understanding of the issues at hand. They actively seek out dissenting opinions and engage in constructive debate because they recognize that the best solutions often emerge from a clash of ideas. Beware the leader who thrives in an echo chamber, surrounding themselves only with yes-men and yes-women who simply echo their own views.

The Power of Persuasion vs. The Power of Substance

Let's face it, some politicians are masters of persuasion. They can deliver a speech that tugs at your heartstrings, leaving you cheering them on. But hold on a second. A captivating speech is all well and good, but can they back it up with substance? Do they have well-researched plans to address the issues they raise? Can they articulate clear solutions and explain how they'll achieve them? Empty promises and emotional appeals are easy. Look for the candidate who can not only inspire but also demonstrate a deep understanding of the complexities of governing.

Media Literacy: Unmasking the Spin

Remember, the media landscape we navigate is not always objective. News outlets can have biases, and social media algorithms can create echo chambers, feeding us information that confirms our existing beliefs. Here's where media literacy becomes crucial. Develop a critical eye. Be aware of potential bias in the information you consume. Seek out diverse viewpoints from reputable sources and don't be afraid to fact-check information before sharing it.

By incorporating these elements, we can move beyond the glitz and glamour of celebrity politics. We can become empowered citizens, equipped to choose leaders who possess not just charisma, but the qualifications, experience, and integrity to truly represent our best interests. In the next chapter, we'll shift gears and dive into the dangers of narcissistic leadership. We'll equip you with the tools to fight back against it, to ensure your voice is heard and your vote truly counts. So, stay tuned, because in the next part, it's all about taking back control and reclaiming your power as a citizen!

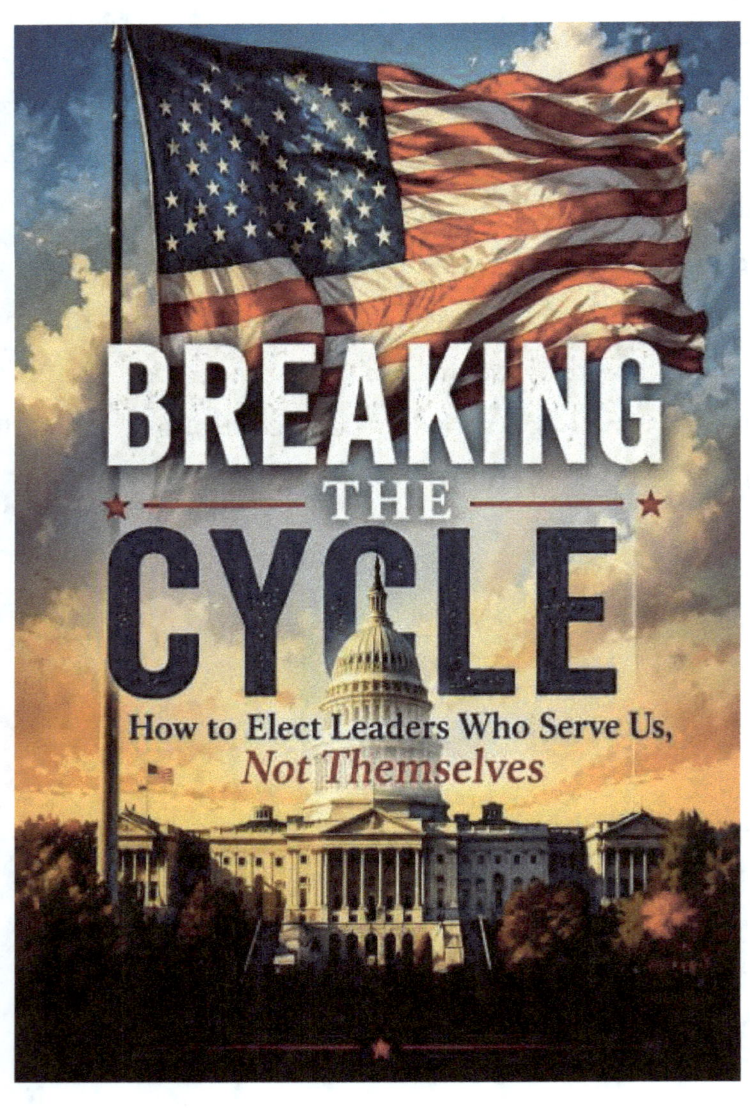

Part 3
Fighting Back: Breaking the Cycle

Chapter 8
The Power of "No"

We've peeled back the layers of celebrity politics, exposing the pitfalls of charisma and the importance of substance in leadership. But awareness is only the first step. Simply recognizing the problem doesn't dismantle it. We, the engaged citizenry, need a toolbox of solutions – ways to hold our elected officials accountable and ensure they represent our best interests, not just their own agendas. This chapter dives into the power of "no," the power of dissent, and the various ways we can make our voices resonate in the halls of power.

From Voting Booth to Public Square: The Spectrum of Active Citizenship

Active citizenship is the cornerstone of a healthy democracy. It transcends the act of simply casting a vote every few years. It's about staying informed, engaging in your community, and making your voice heard – a constant murmur that builds into a powerful roar. There's a wealth of avenues for active citizenship, each catering to different personalities and comfort zones.

The Pen Mightier Than the Soundbite: The Power of Informed Communication

Maybe you're a passionate writer who wields the power of the pen. Craft well-researched letters to your representatives outlining your concerns about specific policies. Don't just express outrage; back it up with facts, statistics, and references to credible news articles or research papers. Frame your arguments not just as emotional pleas, but as well-informed positions supported by evidence.

The Organizer Within: Rallying the Community

Perhaps you're a natural organizer, mobilizing your community through peaceful protests or petition drives. Identify local issues that resonate with you and your neighbors. Organize town hall meetings to discuss concerns and brainstorm solutions. Partner with local advocacy groups like the Sierra Club or the ACLU to amplify your voice and leverage their expertise.

The Digital Soapbox: Social Media and Citizen Engagement

Social media, for all its flaws, can be a powerful tool for

citizen engagement. It allows you to connect with like-minded individuals, amplify your voice, and share information about important issues. However, navigating the digital landscape requires a critical eye. Social media algorithms can create echo chambers, feeding you information that confirms your existing beliefs. Be mindful of these challenges and strive for a balanced perspective.

Here are some tips for responsible social media use:

Follow reputable news sources and journalists. Look for verified accounts with a history of fact-checking and unbiased reporting.

Be wary of sensational headlines and emotionally charged content. Read beyond the headline and fact-check information before sharing it.

Seek out diverse viewpoints. Don't just follow people who agree with you all the time. Engage in respectful discussions with people who hold different perspectives.

Use social media as a springboard for further research. Don't rely solely on social media for information. Consult credible news websites, government reports, and academic journals for a more in-depth understanding of complex issues.

Beyond Likes and Shares: The Art of Effective Communication with Elected Officials

The key is to find what works for you and to be persistent. Don't underestimate the power of a well-written email or phone call to your elected official. Remember, they work for you. Express your concerns in a respectful but firm tone. Be specific about the issue at hand. Don't just say "I'm against this bill." Explain why you oppose it, reference relevant data or news articles, and propose a solution, if possible. Don't be afraid to follow up if you don't receive a response. Persistence shows them that you're serious and that this issue matters to you.

Lessons from History: The Enduring Power of Collective Action

History is peppered with inspiring examples of active citizenship leading to positive change. The Civil Rights Movement of the 1950's and the 1960's stand as a testament to the power of collective action. Through peaceful protests, boycotts, and voter registration drives, millions of Americans raised their voices against racial segregation and discrimination. Their unwavering commitment ultimately led to the passage of landmark legislation that outlawed these practices and paved the way for a more just society.

Case Study: The Water Protectors at Standing Rock

Closer to home, the Dakota Access Pipeline controversy serves as a more recent example of citizen activism holding power to account. The proposed pipeline, which would have disrupted sacred lands and threatened the water supply of the Standing Rock Sioux Tribe, sparked widespread protests in 2016. Thousands of people, both Native American and non-Native American, converged on North Dakota to peacefully demonstrate their opposition. Their unwavering presence, coupled with a relentless social media campaign that prioritized factual information, garnered international attention and pressured the Obama administration to halt construction of the pipeline. While the fight for clean water continues for indigenous communities across the country, the Standing Rock movement serves as a powerful reminder that citizen action can indeed influence the decisions of powerful entities.

Empowering Your Voice: There's a misconception that making a difference requires grand gestures. The truth is, positive change often starts small, with you taking that first step. Whether it's crafting a well-researched letter to your representative or attending a local school board meeting to voice your concerns, you contribute to a more informed citizenry.

Empower yourself: Research organizations like the League of Women Voters or local groups focused on issues you care about. Consider volunteering your time or donating to support their work.

Stay informed: Explore how you can stay up-to-date on current policies – follow reputable news sources, subscribe to issue-specific newsletters from trusted organizations, or engage in respectful discussions with people who hold different viewpoints. Remember, the power lies not in a single act of dissent, but in the collective force of a mobilized citizenry.

So, ask yourself: What effective ways are there to hold officials accountable beyond voting (attending town halls, contacting representatives, supporting good governance organizations)? How can you stay informed about current policies (reliable news sources, podcasts, documentaries)? By harnessing the power of "no" and refusing to be passive bystanders, we can collectively shape the future.

The Ripple Effect: How Our Voices Shape the Future

Just as a single pebble dropped into a pond creates ripples that expand outward, our voices, when raised in unison, can create a wave of change. The power lies not in a single act of dissent, but in the collective force of a mobilized citizenry.

A Bridge to the Next Chapter: The Role of a Free Press

As we've seen, a free and independent press plays a crucial role in holding leaders accountable by shining a light on wrongdoing and keeping the public informed. In the next chapter, we'll dive into the importance of a healthy media landscape in a well-functioning democracy. We'll explore the challenges facing journalism today and discuss how we, as citizens, can support a free and independent press that serves as the watchdog of our government.

Chapter 9
Guarding the Watchdog

A Free Press, a Vital Safeguard

Imagine a world shrouded in shadows, where information trickles down from a single, opaque source. Dissent is a whisper quickly snuffed out, and the truth is a carefully curated narrative. This Orwellian nightmare stands in stark contrast to the vibrant tapestry of a healthy democracy. Here, a free and independent press plays a critical role, acting as a relentless bloodhound sniffing out corruption and abuse of power. It shines a light into the darkest corners, ensuring transparency and safeguarding the public interest. But this vital watchdog faces a multitude of threats in the modern world, threats that we must recognize and combat.

Threats to Press Freedom in the Modern World

The first threat comes in the form of blunt censorship, a tactic often employed by authoritarian regimes. Here, governments wield the power of censorship like a hammer, silencing dissenting voices and controlling the narrative with an iron fist. Imagine news outlets transformed into propaganda machines, churning out carefully crafted messages designed to manipulate public opinion rather than report factual information. This stifles critical thinking, reduces citizens to passive consumers of information, and cripples a society's ability to hold its leaders accountable.

However, even in democracies, a more insidious threat lurks – media consolidation. As a handful of corporations gobble up major news outlets, a disturbing trend emerges: homogenized content and a reluctance to challenge powerful interests. These corporate giants prioritize profit margins over investigative journalism, the very lifeblood of a healthy press. Think of it like a pack of hunting dogs bred for docile obedience, trained not to chase the scent of corruption but to chase the fleeting allure of viral trends and clickbait headlines.

The Power of Investigative Journalism

Thankfully, the spirit of investigative journalism remains alive, a beacon of hope in a media landscape increasingly dominated by corporate interests. These intrepid journalists, fueled by an insatiable hunger for truth, dedicate themselves to unearthing wrongdoing, often at great personal cost. They are the Davids taking on the Goliaths of power, armed not with slingshots but with meticulous research, dogged persistence, and an unwavering commitment to justice. History is replete with examples of these courageous individuals who exposed corruption, even when faced with threats and intimidation.

Case Studies: The Watchdog in Action

Watergate and the Power of Deep Throat: One such example is the iconic duo of Bob Woodward and Carl Bernstein from The Washington Post. Their relentless pursuit of the truth in the Watergate scandal, fueled by anonymous sources known only as "Deep Throat," ultimately led to the resignation of President Nixon. Their tireless investigation shattered the facade of an seemingly untouchable administration, exposing a web of lies and deceit that stretched to the highest office in the land.

The Pentagon Papers and Exposing the Truth: Another powerful example is the case of the Pentagon Papers. These classified documents, leaked by whistleblower Daniel Ellsberg in 1971, revealed a shocking truth: the US government had been systematically misleading the public about the Vietnam War. The publication of these documents by The New York Times and The Washington Post sparked a national debate, forcing Americans to confront the true costs of a seemingly unwinnable war.

Navigating the Information Age

In today's digital age, where information bombards us from social media feeds to news notifications, navigating the media landscape can feel like trying to drink from a firehose. So, how can you identify reliable and trustworthy news sources? Here are some key considerations:

Look for Established Media Outlets with Journalistic Integrity (e.g., The New York Times, The Washington Post, The Wall Street Journal)

Investigate the Ownership Structure of a News Outlet

Be Wary of Sources Reliant on Anonymous Sources or Emotional Language

Cross-check Information with Multiple Reputable Sources

The Dangers of Media Manipulation

The dangers of government censorship and media monopolies are multifaceted and far-reaching. These threats create a breeding ground for misinformation and a culture of blind acceptance. Here's why they are so detrimental:

Stifled Dissent: A free press allows for the expression of diverse viewpoints, even those critical of the government. When dissent is silenced, it becomes impossible to hold leaders accountable.

Erosion of Trust: When the public can't trust the media to

provide accurate information, it erodes trust in all institutions. This can lead to cynicism, apathy, and a decline in civic engagement.

Breeding Ground for Corruption: In the absence of a watchful press, corruption can flourish unchecked. Politicians and corporations may engage in unethical behavior with little fear of exposure.

The Importance of a Free Press

A vibrant, independent press serves as a cornerstone of a healthy democracy. It acts as a vital check on the power of leaders, ensuring transparency and accountability. It empowers citizens to make informed decisions about their representatives and the issues that affect their lives. Imagine a society where citizens are not passive consumers of information, but active participants in shaping their communities and their government. A free press fosters this kind of engaged citizenry, providing the information and critical thinking skills necessary for a functioning democracy.

Supporting Investigative Journalism

Supporting independent journalism initiatives is crucial in maintaining a strong and independent press. Here are some ways you can contribute:

Subscribe to reputable news outlets
Donate to investigative journalism projects
Spread awareness

The Long Road to Change

The reality is that dismantling a corrupt system can be a long and arduous process. Not every situation allows for the immediate removal of a leader, especially if they have consolidated power and control over the media. Imagine a society where the very outlets meant to inform the public are churning out propaganda, drowning out dissenting voices, and painting a rosy picture of a deeply flawed system. In such a scenario, citizens may feel helpless and unsure where to turn.

Strategies for Navigating a Difficult Situation

While the path may be challenging, there are strategies that citizens can employ to navigate a difficult situation with a narcissistic leader and a compromised press:

Seek Out Diverse News Sources: Don't rely solely on mainstream media outlets, especially if they are suspected of being mouthpieces for the regime. Look for independent journalists, bloggers, and alternative media sources that provide critical perspectives. Here's where evaluating sources for credibility becomes important. Look for transparency about their funding sources, a commitment to fact-checking, and a willingness to correct errors.

Embrace Critical Thinking: Don't accept information at face value. Develop your critical thinking skills by questioning the sources of information, analyzing the evidence presented, and considering alternative viewpoints. Look for logical fallacies, emotional manipulation, and hidden biases in the information you consume.

The Power of Community: Connect with like-minded individuals who share your concerns. Form online communities (using encrypted messaging apps if necessary), participate in peaceful protests (if safe to do so), and engage in respectful discussions about the challenges facing your society. Sharing your concerns and collaborating with others can provide a sense of empowerment and solidarity.

Documenting Abuses (with Caution): If possible, document human rights abuses, corruption, and other injustices. This could involve recording protests with body cameras (being mindful of your safety), collecting eyewitness accounts anonymously, or taking photographs or videos of wrongdoing. This documentation can be shared with international organizations, human rights groups, and independent media outlets, helping to expose the truth to a wider audience. Always prioritize your safety and avoid putting yourself in danger.

Maintain Hope and Resilience: The fight for a just and equitable society requires unwavering hope and resilience. There will be setbacks and moments of discouragement, but it's important to maintain a long-term perspective. Remember, even seemingly entrenched regimes can eventually crumble when faced with a persistent and unified citizenry.

The Watchdog Never Sleeps

The fight for a free and independent press is an ongoing battle. New threats emerge, and vigilance is key. By supporting investigative journalism, subscribing to reputable news outlets with journalistic integrity, and developing critical thinking skills, we can become empowered citizens, capable of discerning truth from fiction and holding those in power accountable. Remember, the watchdog never sleeps. It barks the loudest when the need is greatest, reminding us of our responsibility to safeguard the cornerstones of a healthy democracy – transparency, accountability, and the free flow of information.

When a leader prioritizes self-aggrandizement over the needs of the people, the impact can be far-reaching. We dive into the complexities of dealing with a narcissistic leader on a personal level in the next chapter. It explores strategies for managing their manipulative tactics, protecting your own well-being, and ultimately, finding a path towards personal growth and healing.

Chapter 10
Whispering Truth to Power

Imagine a constant state of low-grade anxiety. Every interaction with authority feels fraught, every decision laced with a silent question: will this ruffle feathers or bring down the hammer? This is the reality for many people living under narcissistic leadership. While the dream might be an immediate removal of such a leader, the path to positive change is rarely linear. This chapter dives into navigating this challenging scenario, equipping you with tools for self-preservation and strategies to keep advocating for a better future, even in the face of adversity.

Understanding Narcissistic Leadership

Before we dive in, let's establish a common ground. Narcissistic leaders are often characterized by an inflated sense of self-importance, a constant need for validation, and a disregard for dissenting voices. Their focus may be on self-aggrandizement rather than serving the needs of their followers.

Self-preservation in the Storm's Eye

Living under a narcissistic leader can be emotionally draining. Their constant need for validation and their hair-trigger temperaments can leave you feeling like you're constantly walking on eggshells. The first step to navigating this environment is self-preservation. This doesn't mean rolling over and accepting the status quo; it means setting boundaries and managing your expectations. Recognize that under a narcissistic leader, criticism, even constructive criticism, is unlikely to be well-received. Learn to pick your battles and focus on areas where you can make a positive impact. This might involve compartmentalizing your work life and finding solace in your personal pursuits. Remember, self-care isn't a luxury; it's the fuel that keeps you going in the long run.

Advocacy in a Stifling Climate

So, self-preservation is crucial, but what about actively working for change? The good news is, even under a narcissistic leader, there are still avenues for advocating for positive change. One approach is to support existing opposition movements. Look for groups and organizations that align with your values and offer your time, skills, or resources. If public dissent feels too risky, consider working within the system. This could involve quietly advocating for better policies within your organization or voting strategically in upcoming elections. Local activism is another powerful tool for change. Focus on issues that directly affect your community and start small – organize neighborhood cleanups, petition for improved public services, or attend local government meetings to voice your concerns. Remember, even seemingly insignificant actions can ripple outwards, creating a wave of positive change.

Lessons from the Past: Whispering Truth to Power

History is replete with examples of individuals and groups who dared to speak truth to power, even in the face of immense danger. Take Nelson Mandela and the anti-apartheid movement in South Africa. For decades, they faced brutal repression, yet they persevered. Their unwavering commitment to justice, their strategic use of non-violent resistance, and their ability to garner international support ultimately led to the dismantling of apartheid. This is just one example; countless others exist throughout history – from the Tiananmen Square protests to the Civil Rights Movement in the United States. These stories

serve as a powerful reminder that even in the darkest of times, the human spirit for freedom and justice can prevail.

Case Study: The Water Protectors and the Dakota Access Pipeline

The rise of social media and a growing awareness of environmental issues have empowered grassroots movements in the United States to challenge powerful corporations and even the federal government. One such example is the resistance against the Dakota Access Pipeline (DAPL) led by the Water Protectors, a coalition of Indigenous tribes and their allies.

Donald Trump, who had campaigned on promises of deregulation and energy independence, signed an executive order in 2017 to expedite the construction of the DAPL. This decision was seen by many as prioritizing corporate interests over environmental and Indigenous rights. Trump's rhetoric, often characterized by self-aggrandizement and a disregard for dissenting voices, further fueled the resistance. He dismissed the Water Protectors as "professional protesters" and referred to their concerns as "phony" environmentalism.

The Trump administration's response to the protests was heavy-handed. Law enforcement utilized militarized tactics, including water cannons, tear gas, and rubber bullets against the unarmed protestors. This excessive force drew widespread condemnation and media attention, further galvanizing the Water Protectors' movement.

The Water Protectors: A Model for Resistance

The Water Protectors' resistance against the DAPL serves as a powerful example of how a group can effectively challenge a perceived narcissistic leader. Here's a breakdown of their key strengths:

Unity and Diversity: The Water Protectors' strength lay in their unity, bringing together diverse groups under a common cause.

Non-Violent Resistance: Despite facing brutality, the Water Protectors adhered to peaceful tactics, garnering public sympathy.

Leveraging Technology: Social media played a critical role in spreading awareness

Shifting Public Narrative: By highlighting environmental concerns and Indigenous rights, the Water Protectors challenged the Trump administration's narrative.

Inspired by the Water Protectors' resilience, let's explore ways to translate this hope into action in your own life. Even in challenging times, here are strategies to stay motivated and make a difference:

Hope and Action

Living under a narcissistic leader can be disheartening. News may be filled with negativity, and progress may feel glacial. But it's crucial to hold onto hope. Remember, change, even positive change, rarely happens overnight. So how do you stay motivated? First, find your inspiration. Read stories of successful resistance movements, surround yourself with positive and like-minded people, and focus on the bigger picture – the future you're striving to create.

Now, let's translate that hope into action. Get involved in your local community. Attend city council meetings, volunteer for causes you care about, or simply have conversations with your neighbors about the issues that matter to you. Remember, even seemingly insignificant actions can create a ripple effect.

Leveraging Your Strengths for Change

The beauty of activism lies in its inclusivity. You don't need to be a world-renowned orator or a political strategist to make a difference. Consider your unique skills and resources. Are you a talented writer? Use your words to raise awareness. Are you a skilled organizer? Channel those talents into mobilizing your community. Perhaps you have a knack for social media? Utilize that platform to share credible information and spark discussions. There's a role for everyone in the fight for a better tomorrow.

A Glimpse of a Brighter Future

This chapter has focused on navigating a challenging present, but it's important to remember that this is not the end of the story. Authoritarian regimes, no matter how powerful they may seem, are rarely permanent. History teaches us that even the most entrenched systems can crumble when faced with persistent and unified resistance.

As we move forward, let's envision a future built on different leadership models. Leaders who prioritize empathy and collaboration over self-aggrandizement. Leaders who value diverse perspectives and encourage open dialogue. Leaders who understand that their power comes from serving the people, not the other way around.

This future won't materialize overnight. It will require sustained effort, unwavering commitment, and a willingness to learn from the past. But the rewards are immeasurable – a society where truth is valued, dissent is respected, and the potential of every individual is nurtured. The whispering truth to power, once a risky act of defiance, can become the cornerstone of a more just and equitable world. Let that be the guiding light as you navigate the challenges of the present and work towards a brighter future.

This chapter has equipped you with tools for self-preservation, strategies for advocacy, and a renewed sense of hope. Remember, you are not alone in this fight. There are millions of others who share your desire for positive change.

In the next chapter, we explore the principles of transparency in governance and showcases successful initiatives that foster a sense of trust between leaders and the public.

Chapter 11
Building Trust: The Cornerstone of Good Governance

Imagine a world where cynicism doesn't cloud every interaction with authority. A world where leaders aren't shrouded in secrecy, and citizens aren't left wondering about the motivations behind government decisions. This isn't a utopian fantasy; it's the foundation of a healthy democracy built on trust. Chapter 10 equipped you with tools to navigate challenging leadership, but true progress hinges on building a better future. This chapter dives into the cornerstone of good governance – transparency.

Transparency isn't just a politician's empty promise; it's a multifaceted concept encompassing open access to information, clear communication, and a system of accountability. Think of it as sunlight illuminating the inner workings of government. When citizens have unfettered access to data and policies, they're empowered to participate meaningfully in the democratic process.

Here's the crux: with open access to information, citizens can become informed participants, not passive bystanders.

Imagine the difference between blindly accepting a new policy that reduces funding for public schools and understanding the rationale behind it. Transparency fosters informed participation, allowing citizens to engage in meaningful discourse and hold leaders accountable. It also discourages corruption, as secrecy thrives in the shadows. When government actions are exposed to public scrutiny, the potential for wrongdoing diminishes. Ultimately, transparency strengthens democracy by empowering citizens, promoting accountability, and fostering a sense of shared responsibility for the nation's well-being.

Now, let's turn to some inspiring examples of transparency initiatives closer to home. The United States has a long history of advocating for open government, with several noteworthy programs promoting accessibility. One such initiative is the **Freedom of Information Act (FOIA)**. Enacted in 1967, FOIA allows citizens to request access to information from federal agencies. This empowers individuals to hold the government accountable and ensures a more transparent decision-making process. While there are exemptions to FOIA, it remains a powerful tool for citizens to access government records and shine a light on their activities.

But transparency goes beyond technology. Citizen advisory boards are another powerful tool for fostering open dialogue. These boards, composed of ordinary citizens, provide valuable input on policy decisions. Take, for instance, a transportation committee considering a new bus route. A citizen advisory board, representing diverse voices from the community – students, parents, senior citizens – can offer practical suggestions and ensure that the new route addresses the needs of all residents. This collaborative approach not only increases transparency but also leads to more inclusive and effective policies.

Transparency, however, is just the first step. Effective leadership requires a shift in mindset, moving away from self-promotion and towards collaboration, empathy, and service.

Collaborative leadership styles emphasize teamwork and shared decision-making. Imagine a school principal who convenes meetings with teachers, parents, and students to discuss curriculum changes. By incorporating diverse perspectives, the principal fosters a sense of ownership and increases the likelihood of a successful implementation. No more top-down mandates; collaboration builds trust and leads to better outcomes.

Empathy, the ability to understand and share the feelings of others, is another crucial element of good leadership. A leader who prioritizes empathy considers the needs and concerns of all citizens, not just a select few. Imagine a city council member visiting low-income neighborhoods to understand firsthand the challenges residents face with rising food costs. This act of empathy allows the council member to develop more effective policies to address food insecurity, ensuring no one gets left behind.

Finally, a service-oriented leader prioritizes the public good over personal gain. They understand that their power stems from serving the needs of the people. Imagine a healthcare administrator who works tirelessly to improve access to affordable healthcare for all citizens. This leader isn't motivated by personal glory but by a genuine desire to improve the lives of their community. True leadership isn't about self-aggrandizement; it's about service.

Building successful leadership models that prioritize collaboration, empathy, and service requires a cultural shift.

Educational institutions can play a crucial role by instilling these values in future generations. Public discourse needs to elevate these qualities and hold leaders accountable for upholding them. Citizens can actively seek out information from credible sources, engage in constructive conversations, and participate in the democratic process.

A powerful example of a government initiative that embodies transparency, collaboration, and service is participatory budgeting. This process allows citizens to directly allocate a portion of the public budget. Imagine a community deciding on how to spend funds for a new park. Through participatory budgeting, residents can vote on proposals for playgrounds, walking paths, or even community gardens. This collaborative approach empowers citizens, ensures their voices are heard, and fosters a sense of ownership over public projects. Participatory budgeting isn't just about funding; it's about empowering communities to shape their future.

The Road to a Brighter Future

Transparency, collaboration, empathy, and service – these are the pillars of a healthy democracy. By advocating for greater transparency from our leaders, we can build a future where trust flourishes. Remember, informed citizens are empowered citizens. Let's embrace these principles and work together to build a better future, one where leadership serves the people, not the other way around.

The Roadblocks on the Path

While the benefits of transparency and alternative leadership models are undeniable, achieving them requires acknowledging the challenges that lie ahead. One major hurdle is entrenched interests. Powerful individuals or groups who benefit from the status quo may resist change. Imagine a wealthy oil company that profits from drilling on public lands. They might lobby against environmental regulations, even if such regulations are in the public interest. These entrenched interests can wield significant influence, making it difficult to implement reforms that prioritize transparency and accountability.

Another challenge is media manipulation. In today's information age, citizens are bombarded with news from a variety of sources, not all of them credible. Misinformation and disinformation campaigns can sow discord and undermine trust in institutions. Imagine a social media campaign spreading false information about a new healthcare policy. This can lead to public confusion and hinder informed participation in the democratic process. Countering media manipulation requires critical thinking skills and a commitment to seeking out reliable sources of information.

Overcoming Political Polarization: A Path Forward

Finally, political polarization can further erode trust and hinder progress. When political discourse becomes overly partisan, it becomes difficult to find common ground and work towards solutions. Imagine a deeply divided Congress where gridlock prevents any meaningful legislation from being passed. Overcoming political polarization requires a multi-pronged approach:

Foster Civil Discourse: Encourage respectful dialogue across the political spectrum. Promote platforms and initiatives like citizen forums or moderated online discussions that bring people with differing viewpoints together to discuss important issues.

Support Independent Fact-Checking Organizations: Strengthen the role of independent fact-checkers who can debunk misinformation and promote factual accuracy in political discourse. Organizations like PolitiFact or Snopes can be valuable resources.

Explore Alternative Voting Systems (Consider the Benefits and Trade-Offs): Ranked-choice voting, for example, allows voters to rank candidates in order of preference. This can encourage candidates to appeal to a broader range of voters and discourage negative campaigning. However, it's important to acknowledge that alternative voting systems also have drawbacks, such as increased complexity for voters. Further research and public education are necessary before widespread adoption.

By implementing these strategies, we can begin to bridge the political divide and create a more productive environment for tackling complex issues.

The Power is in Your Hands

Despite the challenges, there are ways for citizens to actively promote transparency, collaboration, empathy, and service in their leaders. Here are a few steps you can take:

Demand Transparency: Hold your elected officials accountable for upholding principles of open government. Contact your representatives, attend public hearings, and ask questions about government spending and policy decisions.

Support Investigative Journalism: A free and independent press plays a vital role in exposing wrongdoing and holding leaders accountable. Subscribe to reputable news organizations and support investigative journalism initiatives.

Embrace Civic Engagement: Don't be a passive observer; get involved in your community. Volunteer your time, attend local government meetings, and participate in public forums.

Promote Critical Thinking Skills: In today's information age, it's crucial to be able to discern fact from fiction. Encourage critical thinking skills in yourself and others. Learn how to identify reliable sources of information and be wary of sensational headlines and social media posts. Media literacy resources from libraries and educational institutions can be helpful tools.

Vote Responsibly: Elections are a cornerstone of democracy. Vote in every election, local and national, and research candidates thoroughly before casting your ballot.

A Call to Action

Building a future based on transparency, collaboration, empathy, and service is a continuous process. It requires constant vigilance and active participation from citizens. But the rewards are immeasurable. A society built on trust fosters innovation, promotes inclusivity, and empowers individuals to reach their full potential. Let's embrace the principles outlined in this chapter and work together to build a brighter future for all.

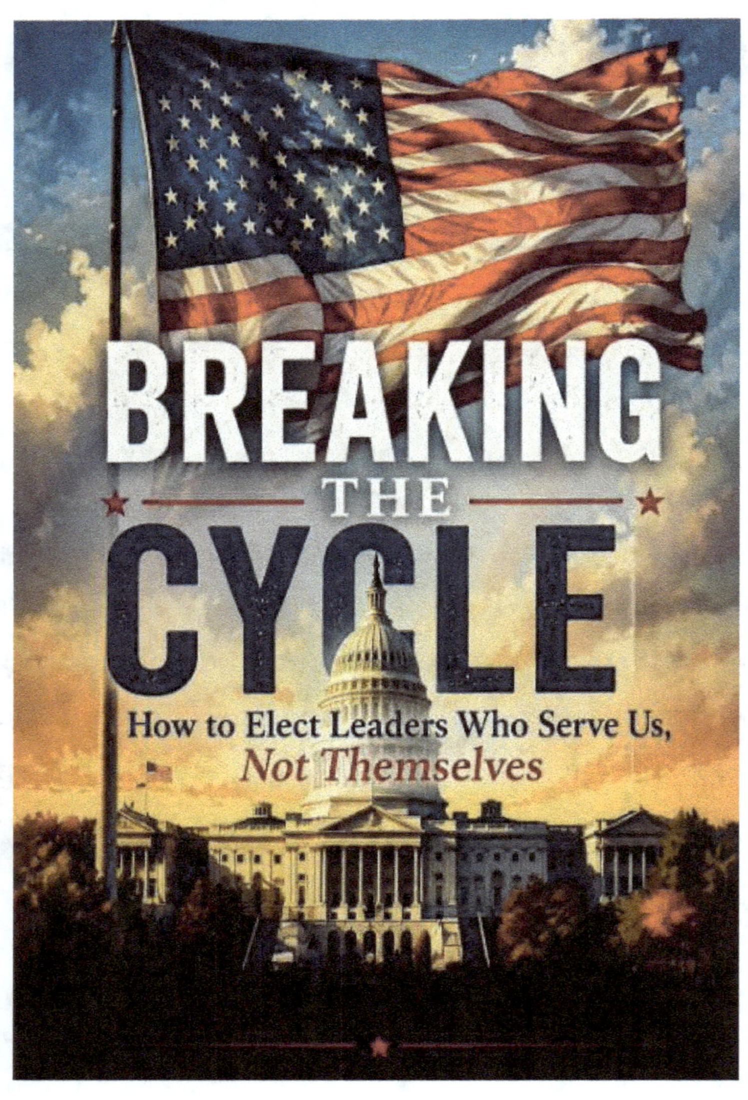
BREAKING
THE
CYCLE
How to Elect Leaders Who Serve Us,
Not Themselves

Conclusion

Empowering the People: A Call to Action

The insidious grip of narcissistic leadership can leave us feeling powerless and demoralized. But within these pages, a different narrative emerges – one brimming with hope and a call to action. This isn't a call for apathy or resignation, but for active participation in building a society where integrity, transparency, and service reign supreme.

We've dived into the complexities of narcissistic leadership, its manipulative tactics, and the devastating consequences it can have. We've learned to recognize the telltale signs, from the insatiable hunger for admiration to the callous disregard for others' well-being. This newfound awareness is the first step towards positive change.

But knowledge without action is like a seed left unplanted. Fostering ethical governance requires an informed, engaged, and empowered citizenry. Education plays a vital role. Revamped curriculums can equip future generations with the critical thinking skills necessary to discern truth from manipulation. Courses in civics and ethics can instill a deep appreciation for democratic values and the importance of holding leaders accountable. Imagine a society where young people are not just passive consumers of information, but active participants in the democratic process – questioning, analyzing, demanding better.

This active citizenry extends far beyond the classroom walls. Civic engagement breathes life into democracy. It's about attending town hall meetings, volunteering in local communities, or simply striking up conversations with neighbors about important issues. These seemingly small acts coalesce into a powerful force, ensuring that the voices of the people are heard.

Leaders Who Inspire Action

But leadership isn't all darkness. history offers us inspiring examples of leaders who governed with humility and integrity. Abraham Lincoln, for instance, led the country through its darkest hour, the Civil War, and still managed to keep his commitment to ending slavery and preserving the Union. His humble beginnings and strong moral compass make him a shining example of ethical leadership.

Barack Obama similarly demonstrated that a leader can be

both strong and compassionate. He worked tirelessly to reform healthcare and address climate change, all while maintaining a sense of empathy and understanding for the American people.

And let's not forget Shirley Chisholm, the first African American woman elected to Congress. She was a trailblazer who fought for education and employment opportunities, and her unwavering dedication to justice and equality continues to inspire us today. These leaders, along with many others, prove that power can be wielded with kindness, compassion, and a genuine desire to serve. They show us that a better tomorrow is possible when leaders put the people first.

The path forward won't be paved with passivity. We must translate knowledge and inspiration into action. The call to action is multifaceted.

Register to vote. This fundamental right is the cornerstone of a healthy democracy.

Research candidates thoroughly. Dive beyond soundbites to understand their values and stances on critical issues.

Support those who champion transparency, accountability, and service.

Local activism offers another avenue for positive change. Whether it's advocating for environmental protection, promoting educational equity, or simply holding local officials accountable for their actions, getting involved can lead to meaningful progress. Don't underestimate the power of your voice. Speak up at public meetings, write letters to your legislators, and hold elected officials accountable for the promises they make.

Staying informed is crucial in this fight. In today's information overload, critical thinking skills are more important than ever. Learn to discern credible news sources from those peddling misinformation. Develop a healthy skepticism towards sensational headlines and social media posts. Seek out diverse perspectives and challenge your own biases.

The Fight for a Better Future

The fight for a better future is a marathon, not a sprint. There will be setbacks, moments of frustration, and times when cynicism may threaten to overshadow our hope. We must persevere. Remember, you are not alone. Millions around the world share your yearning for ethical leadership and a thriving democracy. Together, our collective voices can create a powerful force for change.

Beyond the Fight: Collaboration for Progress

The challenges ahead are significant, but collaboration is a powerful tool. Working within the existing system, advocating for reform, and holding leaders accountable are all crucial steps. We can also support initiatives that promote civic education and media literacy in schools. Imagine a curriculum that equips students with the skills to dissect information, identify bias, and engage in respectful discourse. By fostering a culture of informed participation, we can empower future generations to become active stewards of democracy.

The Future We Choose

Let history not be defined by the narcissistic leaders of the past. Let it be a chronicle of empowered citizens who rose to the challenge, demanding better from those entrusted with power. The future we desire – one built on transparency, empathy, and service – is within reach. Let's claim that future, together. With informed participation and unwavering collective action, we can build a brighter future where ethical leadership flourishes.

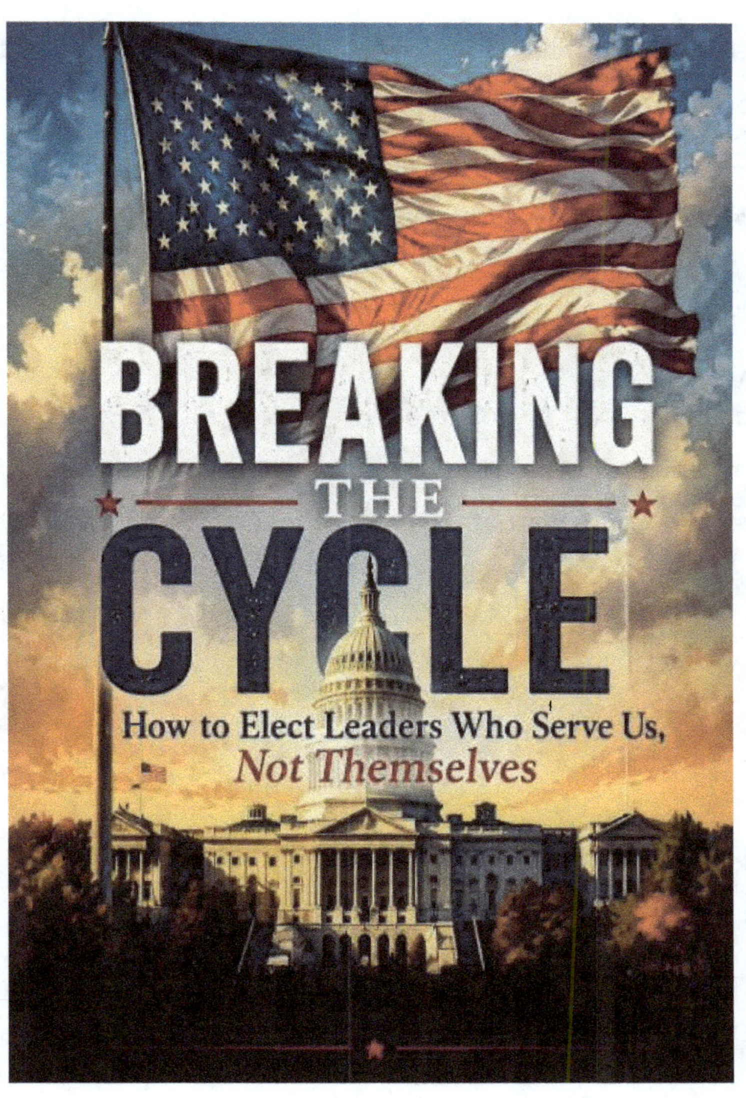

Appendix

Page 117

Further Resources: This appendix provides additional resources for those interested in learning more about narcissistic leadership, good governance, and civic engagement. The information contained herein is for informational purposes only and should not be construed as professional advice.

Disclaimer: The resources listed in this appendix are intended to provide a starting point for further exploration. It is recommended that readers consult with a variety of sources and experts to gain a comprehensive understanding of these topics.

Websites:

Harvard Kennedy School: A leading institution for research and education in public policy and leadership. (https://www.hks.harvard.edu/)

Idealist: This website connects volunteers with opportunities to make a difference in their communities and around the world. (https://www.idealist.org/en/volunteer)

National Conference on Citizenship: This organization provides resources and programs to encourage informed and active citizenship. (https://citizenconnect.us/organization/national-conference-on-citizenship/)

Politico: A news website focusing on politics and policy in the United States. (https://www.politico.com/)

Organizations:

Common Cause: A nonpartisan organization advocating for democracy and good governance. (https://www.commoncause.org/)

Open Secrets: The nation's premier research and government transparency group tracking money in politics and its effect on elections and policy. (https://www.opensecrets.org/)

ProPublica: An independent, non-profit newsroom that investigates abuses of power. (https://www.propublica.org/)

Vote.org: A nonpartisan organization dedicated to increasing voter turnout. (https://www.vote.org)

Books:

"Bowling Alone: The Collapse and Revival of American Community" by Robert D. Putnam: This book explores the decline of civic engagement in the United States and its consequences.

"Democracy in Action: How to Contribute to Building a Better World" by John Keane: This book offers a global perspective on civic engagement and its role in strengthening democracy.

"Good Governance: A Very Short Introduction" by Mark Philpott: This book offers a concise introduction to the concept of good governance and its various dimensions.

"Why Nations Fail: The Origins of Power, Prosperity, and Poverty" by Daron Acemoglu and James Robinson: This book explores the link between governance and a nation's economic success.